Junior
How to Draw
Fairies

Published by Top That! Publishing plc
Tide Mill Way, Woodbridge, Suffolk, IP12 1AP, UK
www.topthatpublishing.com
Copyright © 2013 Top That! Publishing plc
All rights reserved.
0 2 4 6 8 9 7 5 3 1
Printed and bound in China

Introduction

Have you always wanted to draw fairies, but were put off because they looked too difficult? Have no fear! This book shows you a fun and easy way to draw all kinds of fairies—and their magical fairy homes.

Just follow the tips and step-by-step instructions, and you'll soon learn a set of basic drawing techniques that you can then apply to any subject.

Top Tip!

To draw good, clear lines, you need to keep your pencils nice and sharp with a pencil sharpener.

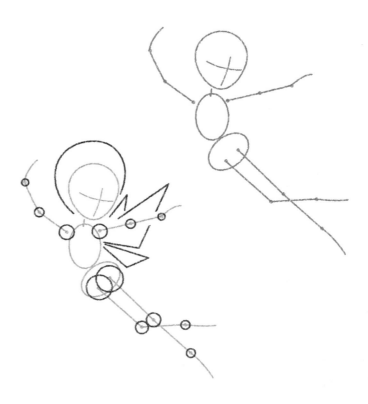

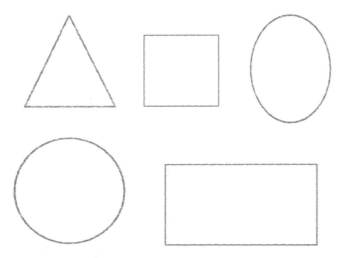

Basic Shapes

When you want to draw something, a good way to start is to look at it carefully and break it down into a series of simple shapes—triangles, squares, rectangles, circles and ovals.

Fairies tend to break down mostly into ovals and circles, with triangles or slanting rectangles for wings. The arms and legs are sketched as dots joined by straight lines (see above).

Notice which shapes are bigger or smaller than others, and where they join together. Look carefully at their angles and proportions. Spend time just looking before you pick up your pencil!

Tools of the Trade

You will need a pencil, an eraser, a pencil sharpener, a ruler, a fine black marker pen and fiber-tip pens or pencils for coloring in your drawings.

A Few Simple Steps

You can apply the "basic shapes" technique to drawing any subject, including fairies. You can use it for simple front-on and side-on views, as well as for more complicated angled views. All it takes is a few simple steps...

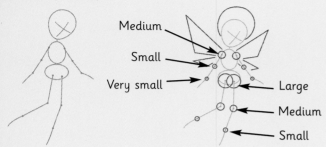

Medium
Small
Very small
Large
Medium
Small

Step 1. Sketch a cross. Draw an egg-shape around it, then two ovals. Draw dots for the limb joints, then join up the dots to show the positions of the arms and legs.

Step 2. Sketch the basic outline for the wings. Circle the dots (limb joints) using four sizes of circle. Make the head larger by adding a crescent.

Step 3. Draw the fairy's outline around the guidelines. Use the cross on the face to help position the eyes, nose and mouth. Add hair.

Step 4. Go over your pencil outline in black pen.

Step 5. Erase the pencil guidelines and color in your magical fairy.

Drawing Faces

The right and left halves of a face should look the same. Use a cross to help you. Position the eyes on the horizontal line of the cross. The vertical line is called the "line of symmetry," and the features should be the same on either side of this line.

For a side-on (profile) view, keep the distances between the eye, nose and mouth the same as for a front-on view.

Proportions

Keep the proportions of the fairy's body the same, whether you are drawing her front-on, side-on or from an angle. The distance from pointed toe to knee, for example, should always be the same as the distance from knee to waist—and the head is always very large!

Front-on View   **Side-on View**   **Angled View**

Tooth Fairy Front-on

If a baby tooth comes out and you leave it under your pillow, the tiny Tooth Fairy may come in the night to collect it! If the tooth has been well cared for, she may leave you a gift. See if you can draw her.

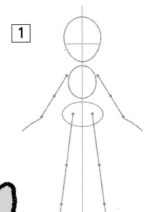

Step 1. First, lightly draw a cross, as shown. Using the cross as a guide, pencil in three ovals—one for the head and two for the body. Next, for each limb, draw three dots to mark the joints. Join the dots to make the legs and arms.

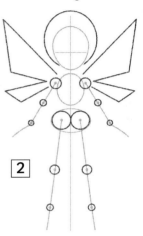

Step 2. Circle each dot, as shown. Use four sizes of circle. Then draw guideline shapes for the wings. Next, sketch a crescent on top of the head to make the head larger.

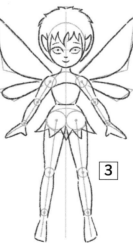

Step 3. Draw a dress on the body. Then sketch the outline of the legs and arms, using the circles as guides. Shape the wings and add detail to the face and hair.

Step 5. Erase the pencil guidelines and have fun coloring in the Tooth Fairy!

Step 4. When you are happy with your Tooth Fairy, go over your pencil outline in black pen.

Tooth Fairy Side-on

Look for fairy dust under your pillow after the Tooth Fairy has been!

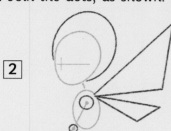

Step 1. Sketch a cross, as shown. Draw an egg-shape around it (make sure the cross is below center). Add two ovals for the body, and a line for the neck. Next, draw three dots for the arm joints and three dots for the leg joints. Join the dots, as shown.

Step 2. Draw circles around each of the dots (use four sizes of circle). Sketch in the basic shapes of the wings and make the head larger by adding a crescent line.

Step 3. Draw a dress on the fairy's body. Then outline her legs, feet, arms and hands, using the circles as guides. Shape the wings and draw her face and hair.

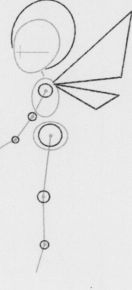

Step 4. Once you are ready to, go over your pencil outline in fine black pen.

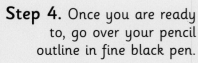

Step 5. Erase any pencil guidelines and color in your lovely Tooth Fairy. To make her wings look delicate and almost transparent, color them pale blue, leaving white highlights.

5

Tooth Fairy from an Angle

Here, the Tooth Fairy is hovering. Can you draw her before she flies away?

Fairy File

Fairies often use leaves, flowers or tiny scraps of cloth to make their clothes.

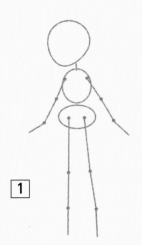

1

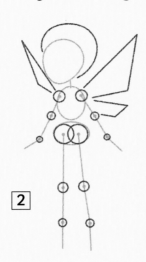

2

Step 1. First, lightly sketch an egg-shape for the head and two ovals for the body. Add a line for the neck. Then draw three dots for the arm and leg joints. Join the dots together to make the arms and legs.

Step 2. Draw a circle around each dot—the biggest circles for the hip joints and the smallest for the wrists. Next, sketch the basic wing shapes. Then draw a crescent around the head to make it bigger.

3

4

Step 3. Next, draw the dress, and then the outline shape of the arms and legs. The fairy's pointed toes makes it look as if she is hovering above the ground. Shape her wings and draw her face, pointed ears and hair.

Step 4. Once you are happy with your drawing, go over your outline in black pen.

5

Step 5. Erase the pencil guidelines and color in your Tooth Fairy. You could always add a little glitter to make her sparkle!

Tooth Fairy Flying

See if you can draw your Tooth Fairy in two different flying positions.

Side-on View

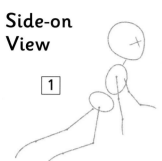

1

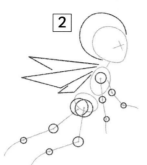

2

Step 2. Circle the dots, as shown. Draw the basic wing shapes, then enlarge the head by adding a crescent line.

3

Step 3. Draw your Tooth Fairy's hair, face and outline, including her dress and wings.

Step 1. Begin by drawing a small cross inside an egg-shape for the head. Next, draw two ovals for the body. Add a neck. Then draw dots for the limb joints —three dots for each limb. Join the dots to make the legs and arms.

4

Step 4. Go over your outline in black pen.

Step 5. Erase the pencil guidelines and color in your flying Tooth Fairy.

5

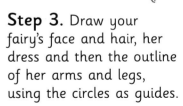

Angled View

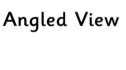

1

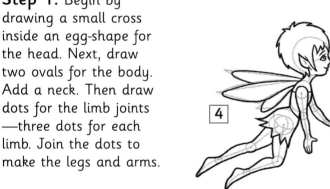

2

3

Step 1. Sketch a small cross. Next, draw an egg-shape for the head, two ovals for the body and a line for the neck. Then draw three dots for the joints in each limb. Join up the dots to make the legs and arms.

Step 2. Circle the joint dots—use four sizes of circle. Sketch the basic wing shapes, then make the head larger by adding a crescent line.

Step 3. Draw your fairy's face and hair, her dress and then the outline of her arms and legs, using the circles as guides.

4

Step 4. Once you are happy with your drawing, go over your outline in black pen.

5

Step 5. Erase the pencil guidelines and bring your magical Tooth Fairy to life by coloring her in.

Woodland Fairy

To draw a Woodland Fairy's face, it helps to use a ruler to get the proportions right!

Front-on View

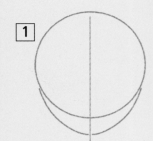

Step 1. Use your ruler to lightly sketch a vertical line. Draw a circle around it, then add a crescent line at the bottom of the circle.

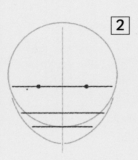

Step 2. Next, draw a horizontal line just below the middle of the circle. Add two dots to mark the position of the eyes. Draw another horizontal line lower down, as shown, and a third line touching the base of the circle.

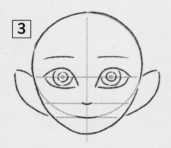

Step 3. Sketch big eyes around the dots. Add the nose on the second line down, and the mouth on the third line. Then draw ears and eyebrows.

Step 4. Add the hair and neck, and go over your outline in black pen.

Step 5. Finally, erase the pencil guidelines and color the face in shades of woodland green!

Fairy File

In folk tales, Woodland Fairies live under trees. They come out at twilight to play, dance, and sing.

Side-on View

Step 1. Draw a circle. Put a vertical line through the middle. Then draw a diagonal line just touching the circle. Add a curved line, as shown.

Step 2. Next, draw three horizontal lines, as shown—one just below the middle of the circle, one lower down, and one touching the base of the circle. Draw in the nose and a dot for the eye.

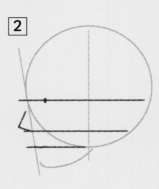

Step 3. Draw the neck, then the large eye and ear. Shape the mouth and add an eyebrow.

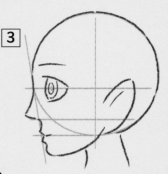

Step 4. Sketch in the hair, then go over your pencil outline in black pen.

Step 5. Erase the pencil guidelines and color in your Woodland Fairy.

Face Looking Up

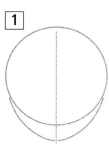

Step 1. Draw a circle. Put a vertical line through the middle. Add a crescent line at the base of the circle.

Step 2. Draw three downward-curving lines on the head shape, as shown, with the top one passing through the middle of the circle. Pencil in two dots for the eyes.

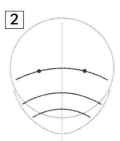

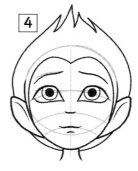

Step 3. Draw the fairy's big eyes. Shape them as shown, with the white of the eye just visible under the iris (the yellow part). Then add the nose, mouth, ears and eyebrows.

Step 4. Sketch in the hair. Once you are happy with your drawing, go over your outline in fine black pen.

Step 5. Gently erase the pencil guidelines and color in your Woodland Fairy.

Face Looking Down

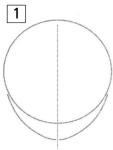

Step 1. Draw a circle. Sketch a vertical line through the middle. Add a crescent line at the base of the circle.

Step 2. Pencil in three upward-curving lines on the head shape, as shown. Draw two dots to represent the eyes.

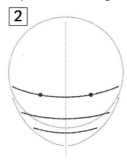

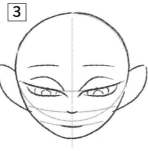

Step 3. Sketch the big eyes looking down— draw the eyelids half closed and only part of the iris visible. Add the nose, mouth, ears and eyebrows.

Step 4. Sketch the fairy's hair, framing the face in a heart shape. Then go over your outline in fine black pen.

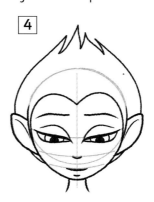

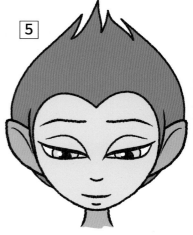

Step 5. Carefully erase the pencil guidelines and color in your fairy.

Face at an Angle

Step 1. Sketch a circle. Add a slightly curved vertical line and a crescent line.

Step 2. Draw three horizontal lines, as shown, and pencil in dots for the eyes.

Step 3. Draw in the neck, then carefully position the big eyes. Add the nose, mouth, ear and eyebrows.

Step 4. Add hair framing the face, then go over your outline in fine black pen.

Step 5. Erase the pencil guidelines and color in your Woodland Fairy.

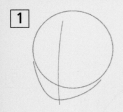

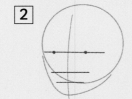

9

Blossom Fairy

Fairies have many animal friends, like this dragonfly, who is giving Blossom Fairy a ride!

Fairy File

With their blue, green or purple bodies and silvery wings that shimmer in the moonlight, dragonflies are quite often mistaken for fairies!

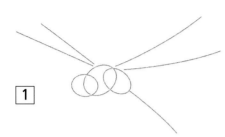

1

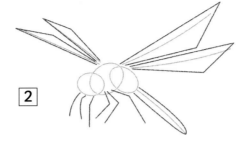

2

3

Step 1. First, lightly sketch three overlapping ovals for the dragonfly's head and body. Add four long lines for the wings and another for the tail.

Step 2. Next, sketch the guideline shapes for the dragonfly's wings and tail, and draw six lines for the legs. Try and match the angles shown here.

Step 3. Now it's time to add the fairy. Start by sketching a small cross inside a circle, for the head. Add two small ovals for the body. Then draw the arms and legs.

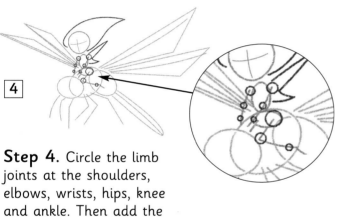

4

Step 5. Draw the dragonfly's face and shape its wings. Then draw the Blossom Fairy's face and the outline shape of her body. Sketch a garland of blossom in her hair!

5

Step 4. Circle the limb joints at the shoulders, elbows, wrists, hips, knee and ankle. Then add the Blossom Fairy's flying hair and her wings.

6

Step 6. Once you are happy with your drawing, go over the outline in fine black pen.

7

Step 7. Erase the pencil guidelines and color in the Blossom Fairy and her dragonfly friend.

Dewdrop Fairy

The Dewdrop Fairy rides his beetle friend like a skateboard!

Fairy File

In the early morning and evening, sparkling droplets of water, or dew, appear on spiderwebs and plants, glittering like diamonds.

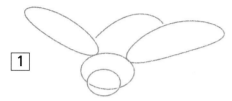

1

Step 1. Sketch the beetle's guideline shapes, as shown. Start with the head.

2

Step 2. Next, sketch the beetle's eyes, antennae, wings and legs.

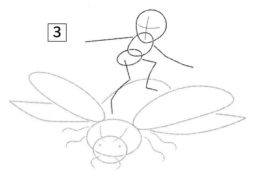

3

Step 3. Time to add the fairy! Draw a small cross inside an egg-shape, for the head. Add two overlapping ovals for the body. Then draw the arms and legs.

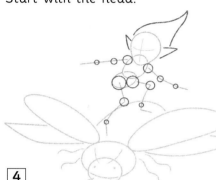

4

Step 4. Draw circles (use four sizes) around the fairy's limb joints at the shoulders, elbows, wrists, hips, knees and ankles. Then give him a pointed hat and ears!

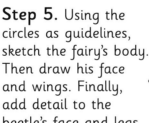

5

Step 5. Using the circles as guidelines, sketch the fairy's body. Then draw his face and wings. Finally, add detail to the beetle's face and legs.

6

Step 6. Once you are happy with your drawing, go over your outline in fine black pen. Add the beetle's wing veins and body stripes.

7

Step 7. Erase the pencil guidelines and color in the Dewdrop Fairy and his beetle friend. Have fun with the colors, and why not add a leafy background?

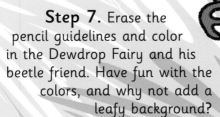

Snail Carriage, Ladybug and Fairy

Fairies are very inventive—this fairy carriage has been made from an empty snail shell! Have fun drawing the fairy, her carriage and her ladybug friend.

Top Tip!

Draw all the characters one by one, but keep in mind the overall composition of the picture by making sure the three drawings are connected. Add an interesting background to really bring your drawing to life.

Snail Carriage

Step 1. Lightly sketch the guideline shapes for the shell, as shown above, starting with the smallest circle and working outward.

Step 2. Next, sketch two circles for the back wheel and two circles for the front wheel. Join them with the curved lines of leaves, as shown. Add another circle for the spiderweb window, and a smaller circle for the fairy's foot-rest.

Step 3. Using the circles of the shell as guidelines, draw a spiral on the shell, and shape its top. Draw an inner circle inside each wheel.

Step 4. Add details to the wheels, the leaves and the spiderweb window, then go over your outline in fine black pen.

Step 5. Erase the pencil guidelines and color in your beautiful snail carriage.

Ladybug

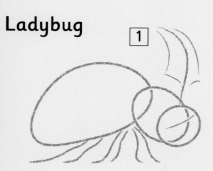 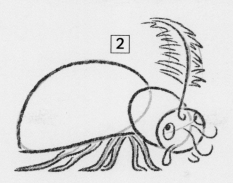 

Step 1. First, lightly sketch an oval for the head. Add a guideline for placing the eyes. Draw two ovals for the body and six lines for the legs. Then sketch the outline of the leaf.

Step 2. Draw the ladybug's outline around your guidelines, then add the eyes and antennae. Next, shape the leaf decoration.

Step 3. Go over your outline in black pen and add the ladybug's spots. Finally, color in your ladybug (see the main picture, below).

Fairy

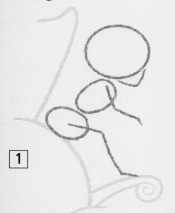 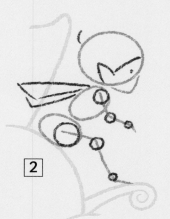  

Step 1. Using the carriage as a position guide, sketch three ovals. Next, draw lines for the lower face and the arm and leg.

Step 2. Circle the limb joints at the shoulder, elbow, wrist, hip, knee and ankle. Then draw the wing shapes and hairline, and a dot for the eye.

Step 3. Draw your fairy's dress, arms and legs. Refine the shape of her wings, face and hairline, and add her mouth.

Step 4. Once you are happy with your drawing, go over your pencil outline in fine black pen—but don't go over the ends of the wings, which are inside the carriage!

Step 5. Erase the pencil guidelines and color in the fairy.

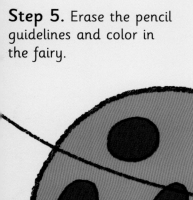  

Mermaid Fairy

Mermaid fairies love to play in the waves and splash each other.

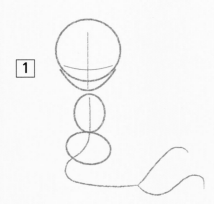

1

Step 1. Draw a circle for the head with a vertical line through the middle. Add an upward-curving crossbar. Then add a crescent line at the base of the circle. Next, draw two ovals for the body. Run a line through the ovals, as shown, and give the line a forked end.

2

Step 2. Draw the outline of the body and tail around your guidelines. Add arms, using dots for joints, and then lines and circles around the dots. Then draw the headdress, hair and wing shapes.

3

Step 3. Next, draw the Mermaid Fairy's face using the cross to help you position the features. Refine the shape of the headdress, wings and hair, and draw her bikini shells. Add a rock for her to sit on.

4

Step 4. Go over your outline in fine black pen and add some fine details.

Step 5. Erase the pencil guidelines and color in your Mermaid Fairy. She'll look really great if you draw some waves splashing onto the rocks.

5

14

Flutter Fairy

The Flutter Fairy is a little clumsy and untidy. She makes a great subject to draw!

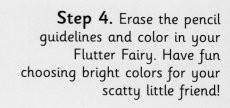

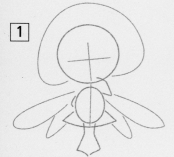

Step 4. Erase the pencil guidelines and color in your Flutter Fairy. Have fun choosing bright colors for your scatty little friend!

Step 3. Add details to the clothes and wings. Then go over your pencil drawing in fine black pen.

Step 1. Sketch a circle for the face and draw a cross inside it. Then sketch the hair shape. Add an oval for the body, a skirt shape, two lines for legs, and finally wings.

Step 2. Draw the Flutter Fairy's face, using the cross as a guide. Add her spiky hair, ears and antennae. Then draw the outline of her body, dress and wings.

Wood Nymph

Wood nymphs live in the trees of the forest and rarely leave their own tree.

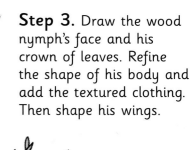

Step 3. Draw the wood nymph's face and his crown of leaves. Refine the shape of his body and add the textured clothing. Then shape his wings.

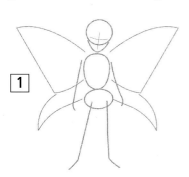

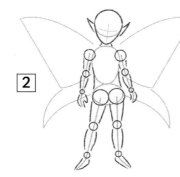

Step 1. Start with the head. Draw a circle and put a cross inside it. Add a crescent line at the base of the circle. Then sketch two ovals for the body, two lines for the arms and another two lines for the legs. Finally, draw the basic shape of the wings.

Step 2. Circle the joints at the shoulders, elbows, wrists, hips, knees and ankles. Use the circles as guides for drawing the outline of the body.

Step 4. Add the finishing touches, such as the wing patterns. Then go over your outline in fine black pen.

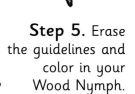

Step 5. Erase the guidelines and color in your Wood Nymph.

Festive Fairy

On an icy winter's day, you may catch a glimpse of the Festive Fairy dancing on a frozen lake.

Fairy File

A circle of mushrooms is called a Fairy Ring, and is a sure sign that there are fairies about! Some say the ring is a gateway to a fairy kingdom.

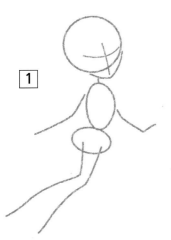

Step 1. First, draw a circle. Put a cross inside it, and add a crescent line at the bottom for the lower half of the face. Next, sketch two ovals for the body. Add a line for the neck, then draw four lines for the arms and legs.

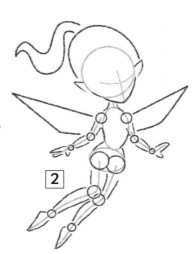

Step 2. Circle the fairy's joints at the shoulders, elbows, wrists, hips, knees and ankles. Use the circles as guides for drawing the fairy's outline. Draw a crescent line for her hat, and add a ponytail. Next, sketch the basic shapes of the wings.

Step 3. Using the cross as a positioning guide, draw the Festive Fairy's face. Give her a crown of holly leaves and berries, and a leafy dress. Curve the edges of her wings.

Step 4. Add further detail to the fairy's hat, leafy dress and stockings, then go over your pencil outline in fine black pen.

Step 5. Finally, erase the pencil guidelines and color in your Festive Fairy. Use festive colors such as red, green and gold. You could even add a wintry background of snowflakes and icicles to make your Festive Fairy feel at home!

16

Fairy Queen

The Fairy Queen rules the fairies. She is clever and kind. Have a go at drawing this beautiful fairy.

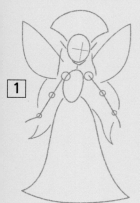
1

Step 1. Draw an oval and put a small cross inside it. Add a crescent line for the lower part of the face, and lines for the ears and hair. Next, draw an oval for the body and a line for the neck. Sketch a long, flowing skirt. Draw joint dots for the arms. Join up the dots and circle them. Then draw the wings and crown.

Step 2. Draw the Fairy Queen's outline around your guidelines. Shape her wings, crown and dress. Then draw her face, using the cross as a positioning guide.

2

3

Step 3. Build up the detail, then go over your outline in fine black pen.

Step 4. Erase the pencil guidelines and have fun coloring in the Fairy Queen.

4

Sundance Fairy

At sunrise and sunset, look for the Sundance Fairy skipping and dancing in the sunbeams.

Step 1. Start by sketching the guidelines shown here. Use an upward-curving crossbar for the cross on the face, as this fairy is looking up.

1

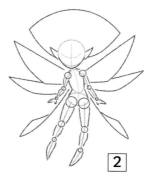

Step 2. Circle the fairy's joints and use the circles as guides for drawing the outline of the body. Add the basic shapes of the wings and headdress.

2

Step 3. Refine the shape of the wings, and give the headdress and boots flame-like edges. Draw in the face, using the cross as a positioning guide.

3

4

Step 4. Add further detail and fiery decoration. Then go over your outline in black pen.

5

Step 5. Erase the pencil guidelines and color in the Sundance Fairy, using yellow, orange and red.

17

Fairy Glade

Now that you've learned how to draw fairies, see if you can create this magical fairy glade and little house. Practice the separate parts first, then put them together to make a scene.

Acorn

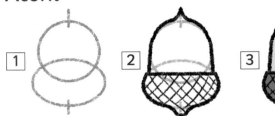

Step 1. First, lightly sketch the guidelines as shown.

Step 2. Draw the outline in pen, and add the diamond shapes to the cup.

Step 3. Erase the guidelines and color in.

Daisy

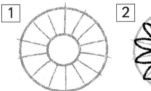  

Step 1. Sketch two circles, one inside the other, and add dividing lines, as shown.

Step 2. Draw a petal around each of the dividing lines. Go over your outline in black pen.

Step 3. Erase the guidelines and color in your daisy.

Toadstool

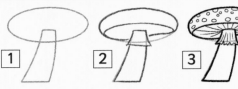

Step 1. Sketch these two simple shapes.

Step 2. Draw the toadstool's outline.

Step 3. Add the spots and frill, and go over in pen.

Step 4. Erase the guidelines and color in.

Buttercup

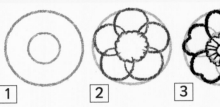

Step 1. Sketch two circles, as shown.

Step 2. Draw five petals around the smaller circle.

Step 3. Add detail, then go over in pen.

Step 4. Erase the guidelines and color in.

Bluebell

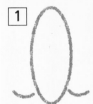  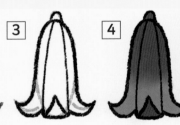

Step 1. Sketch an oval and two curved lines.

Step 2. Draw the petals and top.

Step 3. Go over your sketch in black pen.

Step 4. Color in, making the folded-back petal darker.

House

1

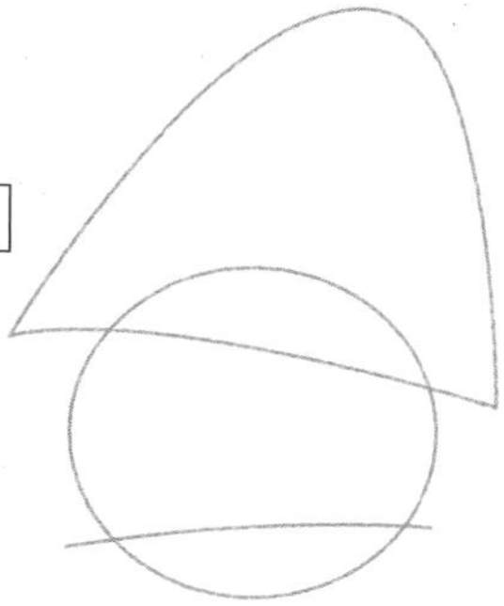

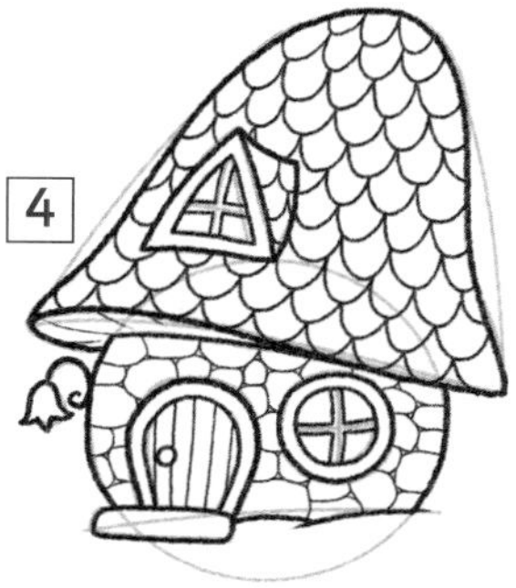

Step 1. First, draw a circle and a cone shape for your guidelines. Draw a line near the bottom of the circle.

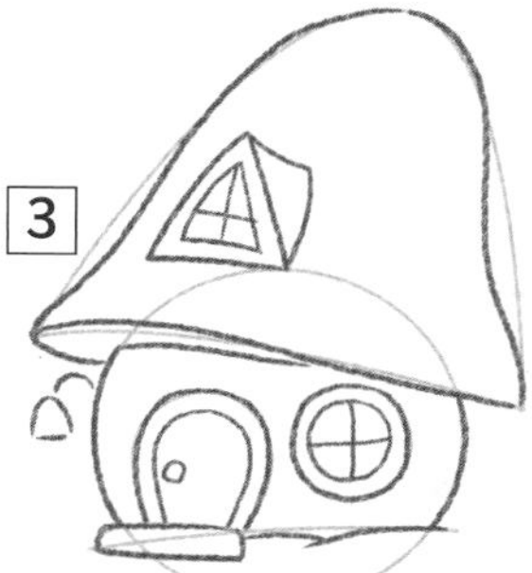

2

Step 2. Using the circle and line as guides, pencil in the door and windows, as shown.

3

Step 3. Add detail to the door and windows, and shape the roof. Draw a little light beside the door.

4

Step 4. Finish by drawing the roof slates and the stones. Once you are happy with your drawing, go over your outline in black pen.

5

Step 5. Erase the pencil guidelines and color in your fairy house. Have fun drawing a background, too, like the one in this picture! Try adding steps leading up to the house, and have a go at the tree roots and secret fairy door.

Fairy Godmother

A fairy godmother has the magical power to grant wishes with a wave of her fairy wand!

3

Step 3. Add the finishing touches, then go over your pencil outline in fine black pen.

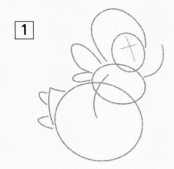

Step 1. First, lightly sketch a small cross inside an oval for the head. Add two more ovals for the body. Next, draw a crescent line for the hair, then sketch in the wings, skirt-tail, arms and feet.

Step 2. Draw your fairy godmother's outline around your guidelines. Then, using the cross as a guide, pencil in her face. Add details to her dress, shape her hair and give her a fairy wand.

Step 4. Erase the pencil guidelines and color in your kindly fairy godmother.

Fairy Princess

The beautiful fairy princess has long, golden hair. She lives in a castle with her magical pet unicorn.

Step 4. Erase the pencil guidelines and color in your beautiful fairy princess in magical colors!

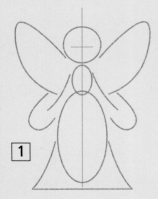

Step 1. Draw a long vertical line (a line of symmetry) and add a short crossbar. Next, sketch a circle for the head and two ovals for the body. Add arms, wings and skirt-tails.

Step 2. Draw the outline of your princess around your guidelines. Include flowing hair and a crown. Use the crossbar to position her eyes.

Step 3. Add detail to your fairy's face and costume—such as a sparkling necklace and long gloves. Then go over your pencil outline in black pen.

20

Fairy Castle

This magnificent fairy castle sparkles in the sunlight. At the end of the year, the fairies gather here for a spectacular winter ball.

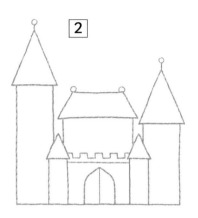

1

Step 1. Using a ruler, draw a horizontal line for the bottom of the castle. Next, draw a large rectangle for the gatehouse wall, and two smaller rectangles for turrets. Top each turret with a triangle. Add the battlements and sketch in the huge doors.

2

Step 2. Next, add two more turrets—one large and one medium-sized— beside the smaller ones. Draw another wall behind the battlements and give it a roof, as shown. Add decorative circles to the top of the large turrets and the roof.

3

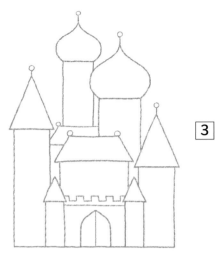

Step 3. Next to the medium-sized turret, draw a tall tower topped by an onion-shaped dome. Add another bit of wall and roof, and above it draw a taller, thinner tower and onion-dome. Top the towers and roof with decorative circles.

4

Step 4. Go over your outline in black pen and add some details, such as flags, windows, door handles and brickwork.

5

Step 5. Erase your pencil guidelines and color in your fabulous fairy-tale castle.

Spring Fairy

Many fairies make beautiful clothes from flower petals and leaves. Try cutting up photographs or snipping out pictures from a magazine so you can dress your own Spring Fairy!

Step 1. Ask an adult to help you take some photographs of flowers and butterflies. Alternatively, snip out pictures from a magazine. Choose flowers that are the right shapes to make good clothes or hats.

Step 2. Using the skills you have learned in this book, draw your own Spring Fairy, but without wings. Use a cross as a guideline for positioning her eyes, and draw dots and circles as guides for the arms and legs. Cut her out.

Step 3. Carefully cut out your flower and butterfly pictures. Stick the butterfly wings onto a piece of paper, then stick your cut-out fairy on top. Add the petals last.

Step 4. Once you have dressed your Spring Fairy, you could cut her out and stick her on a card to send to a friend!

Fall Fairy

Fall fairies wear lovely red and gold leaves, and put bright red berries in their hair. Have fun decorating your own Fall Fairy with cut-out pictures of leaves, seeds and berries.

Top Tip!

Collect real leaves and seeds to stick on to your fairy picture. But leave the berries and insects alone.

Step 1. With the help of an adult, take some photographs of fall seeds, berries, leaves and dragonflies. Alternatively, snip out pictures from a magazine. Choose leaves and seeds that are the right shapes to make good clothes or hats.

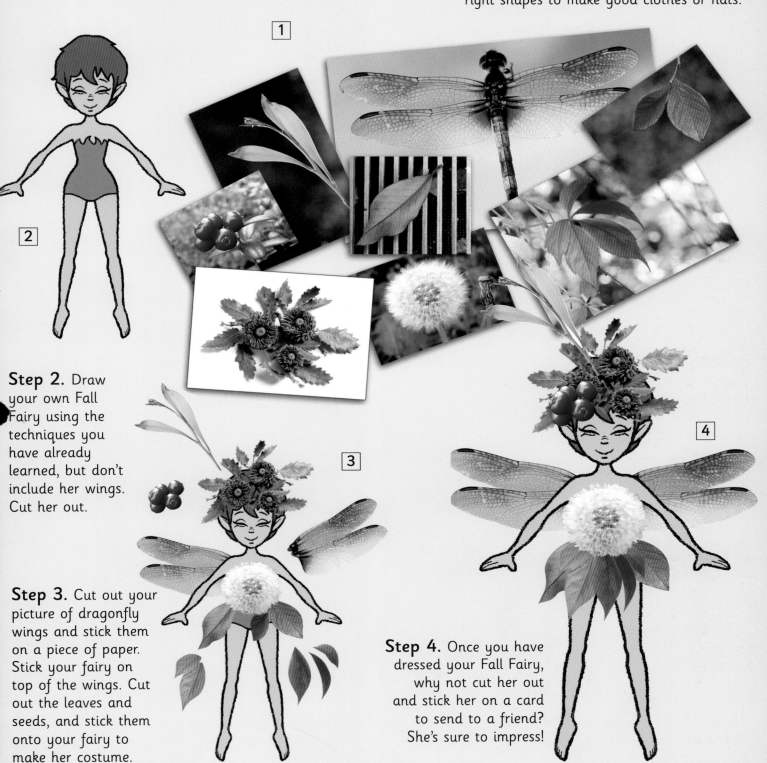

Step 2. Draw your own Fall Fairy using the techniques you have already learned, but don't include her wings. Cut her out.

Step 3. Cut out your picture of dragonfly wings and stick them on a piece of paper. Stick your fairy on top of the wings. Cut out the leaves and seeds, and stick them onto your fairy to make her costume.

Step 4. Once you have dressed your Fall Fairy, why not cut her out and stick her on a card to send to a friend? She's sure to impress!

23

Conclusion

The more you practice, the easier your drawing will become.

Now that you have drawn all the pictures in this book, why not have a go at doing some stunning drawings of your own?

Think of a fairy you would like to draw—she could be a character from a story. Try to see her in your mind as a series of basic shapes. Think about her proportions and the angles of her arms and legs.

If you are copying from a picture or drawing a model, remember always to draw what you can actually see, not what you think something looks like!

Now, take out your sketch pad, pencils, a sharpener, an eraser and a pen—**and get drawing!**

Drawing Cartoon Faces

To draw different expressions, all you need to do is change the shape of the eyes, eyebrows and mouth—their proportions remain the same. Make faces in a mirror and study the effects!

Have fun drawing a range of different expressions. With this skill, you'll be able to illustrate your very own fairy story!

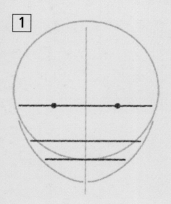

Step 1. Start by drawing a circle with a vertical line through the middle and a crescent line under the circle. Next, draw three horizontal lines, as shown. Add two dots to mark the position of the eyes.

Laughing

Face 1. Draw the eyes shut, eyebrows raised and mouth open.

Sad

Face 2. Draw both the eyebrows and mouth sloping downward.

Shocked

Face 3. Draw eyebrows raised, irises surrounded by white and mouth open.

Thinking

Face 4. Draw one eyebrow raised, eyes looking up and the tip of the tongue out.

Scared

Face 5. Draw eyebrows uneven, small irises and mouth curved downward.

Confused

Face 6. Draw eyebrows uneven, tops of eyes sloping down and lip raised.